better **because...** of Friends

better because™ of Friends

A LITTLE BOOK of GRATITUDE

Cathy Haffner

Better Because...of Friends

For more information,
or to locate a store near you, visit:
www.BetterBecause.com

www.madisonparkgroup.com

better **because...** of you

WITH LOVE FROM:

my life is **BETTER**
because of you

YOU ARE

a wonderful

FRIEND

YOU BRING

FUN

to my life!

no matter the distance
between us or the
time that passes,
our **FRIENDSHIP** continues

you ARE A GREAT inspiration TO **ME**

YOU are there for **ME** when things get tough

YOU ACCEPT me
for who i am

What I **APPRECIATE** most about you is:

you bring

JOY

to so many!

I **LAUGH**
when I think of:

It's nice to know
THERE ARE
PEOPLE LIKE **you**
in this world

you give me

THAT LITTLE **nudge**

when I need it

I CAN **TRUST** YOU
to be honest with me
and keep my secrets

You help me

SEE THE good

in others

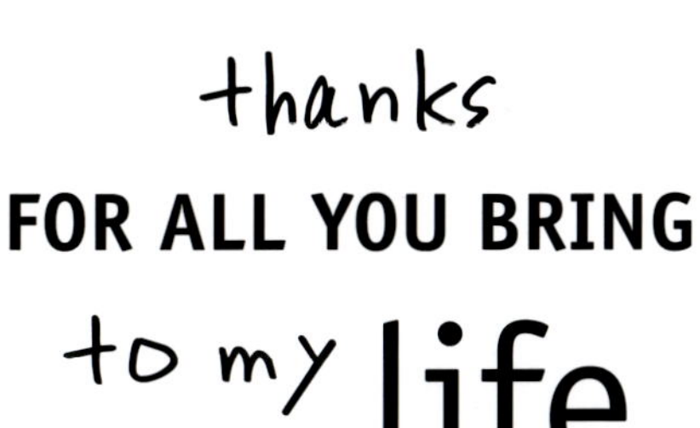
thanks
FOR ALL YOU BRING
to my life

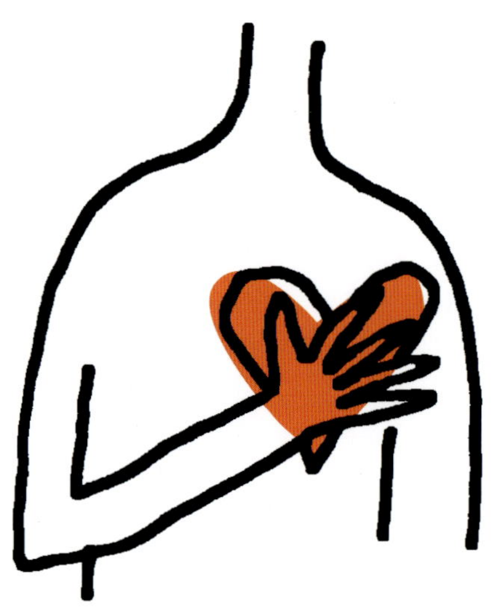

you

WILL **ALWAYS** BE

a special friend

YOU CAN
DO IT!

THANKS FOR
finding the right words
when I need them

WISDOM

What I've **LEARNED** from you is:

FRIENDS
LIKE you
are **WONDERFUL!**

I love how you

EMBRACE LIFE!

you help me
to see what's
good
in my life

I look up to YOU!

YOU'RE amazing!

THANKS

for being a

GREAT FRIEND!

If this book has made
your life a little better,
please share your story with us:

BetterBecause.com
Facebook.com/BetterBecause

Or email me at:
Cathy@BetterBecause.com

About the Author

Cathy believes that "Life's an adventure!" Besides being a leadership coach, she relishes time with family and friends in San Antonio, Texas, and enjoys the majestic mountains and calming waters of the Pacific Northwest.

About the Illustrators

These whimsical works of art were created by Kath Walker and Kasey Free.

Kath is from the U.K. and enjoys chocolate.

Kasey is from Seattle and enjoys travel, sweets, and the sea.

About the Editor

This little book of inspiration was edited by Cathy's friend, Nancy Roberson Davis, who has a big heart and a great talent for words. Cathy is blessed to have Nancy in her life.

The Better Because Collection

is now available in the following titles
By Cathy Haffner:

Better Because…of Mom
Better Because…of Dad
Better Because…of Grandparents
Better Because…of Sons
Better Because…of Daughters
Better Because…of Friends

And, the book that started it all:
Better Because of You
by Cathy & her friend, Ginny Hutchinson